T0011318

BASKETBALL

SCORE WITH STEM!

By K. C. Kelley

Consultant: Tammy Englund, science educator

BEARPORT
PUBLISHING

Minneapolis, Minnesota

Credits

Cover and Title Page, © Alter-ego/Shutterstock; Background image, © Vera Larina/Shutterstock; 4, © GreenLand Studio/Shutterstock; 5 © Focus on Basketball; 6 © Es Sarawuth/Shutterstock; 7 © Boris Ryaposov/Shutterstock; 7 inset © Bonita R. Cheshier/Shutterstock; 8 © Ljupco Smokovski/Shutterstock; 9 © Dmitry Niko/Shutterstock; 10 top © Michael Tureski/Icon Sportswire/Newscom; 11 (2) © Nicholas Piccillo/Shutterstock; 12 Courtesy Nike; 13 © NaturSports/Shutterstock; 14 bottom Courtesy Nike; 14 top © NaturSports/Shutterstock; 15 top © FeatureFlash Photo Agency/Shutterstock; 15 left and bottom © Brian Rothmuller/Icon Sportswire/Newscom; 16 © ImaginStudio/Shutterstock; 17 © Ilya Kovshik/Shutterstock; 18 © Sundry Photography/Shutterstock; 19 © Eric Risberg/AP Photo; 20–21 © Louis Lopez/Cal Sport Media/AP Images; 22 © Pabkov/Shutterstock; 23 © Brian Rothmuller/Icon Sportswire/Newscom; 24 bottom © Cal Sport Media/Alamy; 24 top © UPI/Alamy; 25 © Patrick Schneider/KRT/Newscom; 25 inset © Icon Sports Media/Newscom; 26 © Sports Images/Dreamstime.com; 27 © Quinn Harris/Icon Sportswire/Newscom

Bearport Publishing Company
Minneapolis, Minnesota
President: Jen Jenson
Director of Product Development: Spencer Brinker
Senior Editor: Allison Juda
Associate Editor: Charly Haley
Designer: Colin O'Dea

Produced by Shoreline Publishing Group LLC
Santa Barbara, California
Designer: Patty Kelley
Editorial Director: James Buckley Jr.

Library of Congress Cataloging-in-Publication Data

Names: Kelley, K. C., author.
Title: Basketball : score with STEM! / K.C. Kelley.
Description: Minneapolis, MN : Bearport Publishing Company, 2022. | Series: Sports STEM | Includes bibliographical references and index.
Identifiers: LCCN 2021001080 (print) | LCCN 2021001081 (ebook) | ISBN 9781636911809 (library binding) | ISBN 9781636911878 (paperback) | ISBN 9781636911946 (ebook)
Subjects: LCSH: Basketball--Juvenile literature. | Sports sciences--Juvenile literature.
Classification: LCC GV885.1 .K45 2022 (print) | LCC GV885.1 (ebook) | DDC 796.323--dc23
LC record available at https://lccn.loc.gov/2021001080
LC ebook record available at https://lccn.loc.gov/2021001081

For more information, write to Bearport Publishing, 5357 Penn Avenue South, Minneapolis, MN 55419. Printed in the United States of America.

Contents

Basketball and STEM

The Los Angeles Lakers need one more shot. Luckily, the ball is in the hands of superstar LeBron James. He has amazing skills. And whether he knows it or not, he is going to use STEM to score!

James pushes off the floor with his powerful legs. He seems to float as he flies toward the basket. At just the right second, he lets go of the ball. It swishes into the basket as the buzzer sounds! The game is over. The Lakers—and STEM—win again!

SCIENCE: From flying through the air to bouncing on a court, a basketball moves according to the rules of physics.

TECHNOLOGY: Discover how wearable tech and digital recordings tell us more about the game.

ENGINEERING: **Arenas** are designed to help fans enjoy games in new and exciting ways.

MATH: Information about teams and players is gathered as numbers called **stats**. A winning score is just the beginning!

LeBron James uses science with every shot.

What Goes Up

The point guard sees the clock winding down. Leaping straight up, she snaps her wrist to shoot the ball. It travels in a long, high **arc** before landing in the basket. *Swish!* Three points for the win!

Long-distance shooters make their baskets thanks to lots of practice. But they also have physics to thank. Why?

*Scientists have found that shooting the ball at an **angle** of 30 to 35 degrees from the floor works best for most shots.*

30°

The Perfect Arc

The path a ball travels depends on the amount and direction of the **force** applied to it. A player needs to push the ball upward hard enough to overcome **gravity**. The ball also has to travel at just the right angle to reach the basket.

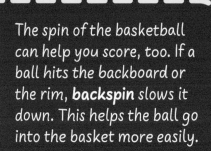

The spin of the basketball can help you score, too. If a ball hits the backboard or the rim, **backspin** slows it down. This helps the ball go into the basket more easily.

Jumping for the Shot

The star player has a chance to score. Will she take a jump shot? Go for a slam dunk? She decides on a layup. She runs forward and jumps, floating the ball straight up. It bounces off the backboard and through the rim—two points!

Professional players can make a layup look easy, but it takes a lot of work. A good layup also relies on physics! Let's see why.

Lay Up, Not Out

To make a layup, a player doesn't throw the ball forward. Instead, she tosses it straight up while running forward. The movement of her body moves the ball, too. As the player tosses the ball up, a force called **inertia** keeps the ball moving forward toward the basket.

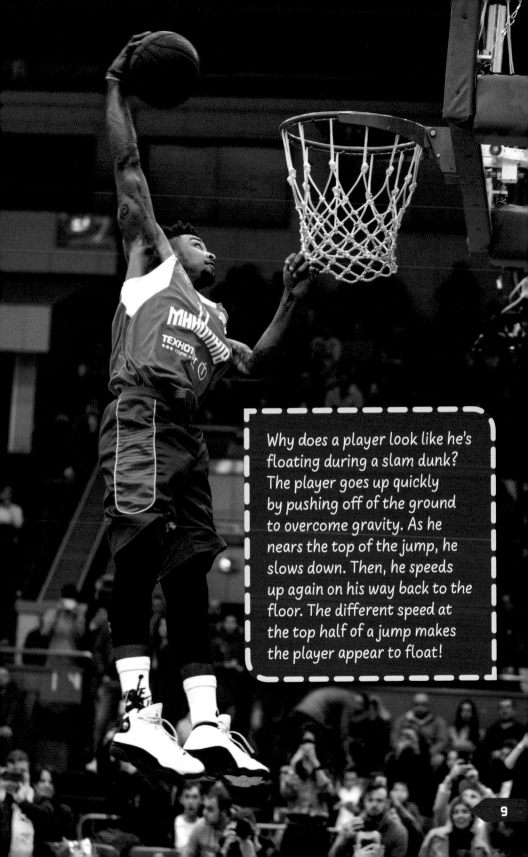

Why does a player look like he's floating during a slam dunk? The player goes up quickly by pushing off of the ground to overcome gravity. As he nears the top of the jump, he slows down. Then, he speeds up again on his way back to the floor. The different speed at the top half of a jump makes the player appear to float!

Make the Right Pass

The point guard stops his dribble and sees an open teammate. He pushes the ball out toward the player. After a quick bounce, the ball lands perfectly in his teammate's hands. How did it get there? Let's look to science for the answer.

This basketball pass bounces up at the same angle as it bounces down.

Angle Matters

The bounce pass is one of the first things basketball players learn. A player pushes the ball toward the ground and it bounces back up to a teammate. The angle at which a ball is pushed down will equal the angle of the ball coming up. If the angle is too high, the ball will go over the teammate's head. A ball at an angle that is too low will end at the teammate's leg.

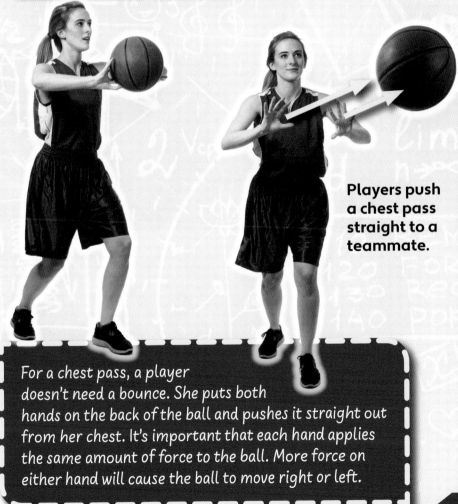

Players push a chest pass straight to a teammate.

For a chest pass, a player doesn't need a bounce. She puts both hands on the back of the ball and pushes it straight out from her chest. It's important that each hand applies the same amount of force to the ball. More force on either hand will cause the ball to move right or left.

Info Everywhere

Millions of fans enjoy watching basketball. They love the fast action, the amazing shots, and the incredible athletes. Announcers provide fans with stats and information both in arenas and on TV. And today's hoops lovers learn more than ever before because of technology worn by the players.

Wearable Tech

Special **sensors** can be put in players' uniforms and shoes to record thousands of pieces of information during a game. The sensors send the information to a computer. Then, coaches and players can use the **data** gathered from this wearable technology to improve.

Sensors in sneakers have to be made strong enough to survive game-day action.

It Starts with the Shoes

A player starts to dribble the ball up the court. Suddenly, she yells, "Time out!" and the game stops. "My shoelaces are loose." She quickly pulls out her phone and taps through an app. "There—laces tightened." And the game is back on.

Tightening with Tech

Technology built into some of the latest shoes can tighten laces for players. Phone apps or buttons on the sides of the shoes make it a snap. In a few taps, the shoes adjust themselves to a perfect fit.

Companies use technology to create new kinds of shoes every year. Some people known as sneakerheads collect as many of these new shoes as they can. National Basketball Association (NBA) player P. J. Tucker *(right)* says he owns more than 2,000 pairs! Fellow NBA star Montrezl Harrell is also a sneakerhead. He wears one pair in the first half of a game and another pair in the second half. He never wears the same pair twice!

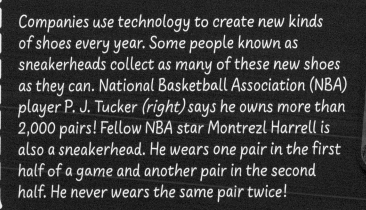

In the pros, some players wear custom-made shoes decorated with colorful designs and artwork.

Smile for the Camera

Pro players are used to being on camera. TV cameras follow every move that the stars make on the court. But these aren't the only cameras pointed at the players. Up in the rafters, there are six **high-resolution** cameras also recording the action.

High-Speed Info

The SportVU camera system collects 25 images per second to record ball and player movement. Then, special software uses the images to provide an incredible amount of information. Teams, coaches, players, the **media**, and fans can use this data to learn more about the amazing sport.

Digital cameras like this one record every movement on the court.

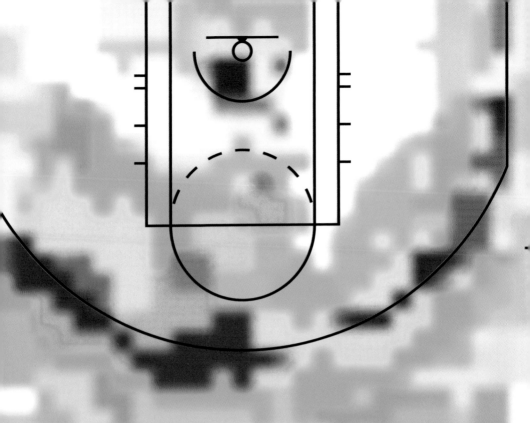

What kind of information does the SportVU collect? One colorful example is a heat map like this one. The cameras gather information on where players take shots. Reds and greens show where shots were successful. Blues show where players made fewer shots. Some information is even available right away during games, so players and coaches can see game data on tablet computers during timeouts.

Building a New Arena

While pro basketball teams have great gear and coaches, they also need places to play. Today's arenas are **engineered** to be better than ever. The owners of the Golden State Warriors spent more than $1.4 billion on a brand new arena, Chase Center. They wanted it to be the best and most modern in the league.

Built for the Future

San Francisco's Chase Center was made with environmentally friendly materials. Almost all of the materials came from nearby. The building's construction was designed to save both water and electricity. To encourage fans to use **mass transit** instead of driving cars, there are only 950 parking spaces for more than 18,000 fans.

Fans at Chase Center can use their smartphones to see videos, stats, and images displayed right on the court!

High above the court at Chase Center is a huge box covered by 9,699 square feet (898 sq m) of screens. The arena's scoreboard is the biggest in the NBA. Engineers designed a support structure to hold up the weight of 165,000 pounds (78,842 kg). It can even be raised or lowered!

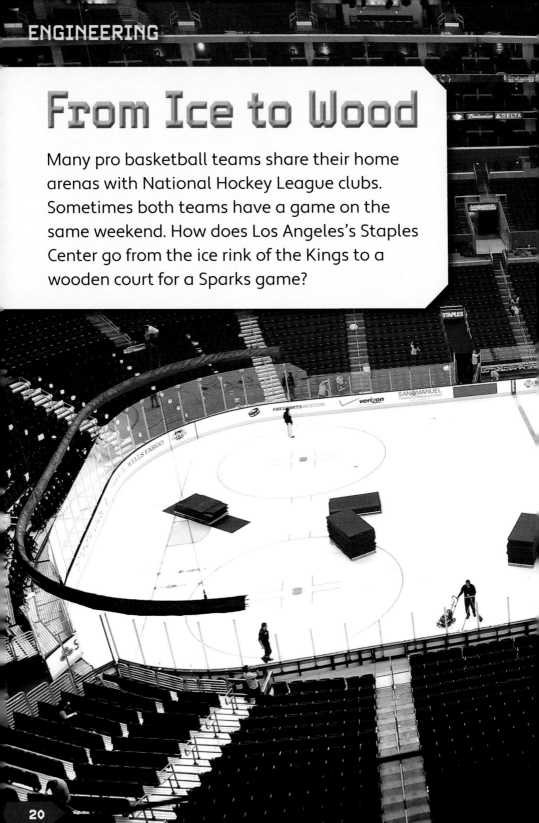

From Ice to Wood

Many pro basketball teams share their home arenas with National Hockey League clubs. Sometimes both teams have a game on the same weekend. How does Los Angeles's Staples Center go from the ice rink of the Kings to a wooden court for a Sparks game?

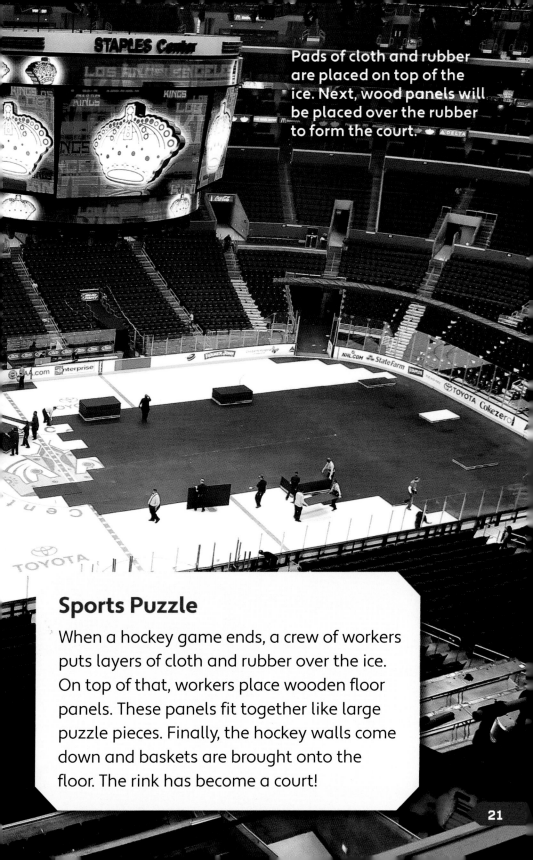

Pads of cloth and rubber are placed on top of the ice. Next, wood panels will be placed over the rubber to form the court.

Sports Puzzle

When a hockey game ends, a crew of workers puts layers of cloth and rubber over the ice. On top of that, workers place wooden floor panels. These panels fit together like large puzzle pieces. Finally, the hockey walls come down and baskets are brought onto the floor. The rink has become a court!

Add 'Em Up!

It's Game 5 of the playoffs. The forward leaps up with the ball. He hovers for a moment high above the rim. Then, he slams it home for 2 points to give his team a 13-point lead, 98–85, with less than a minute left in the 4th quarter. Look at all those numbers from just a single play!

Math Makes the Stat

In sports, numbers are used to record almost every event—points, assists, rebounds, steals, minutes, and games played. These numbers all provide information about the sport. They are called statistics, or stats. Keeping track of all those stats means using a lot of math.

Addition is used in basketball to count points, assists, and more. Division helps find per-game **averages**. Percentages show how successful players are at shooting or rebounding.

Stats are displayed on scoreboards during a game.

Russell Westbrook got 42 triple doubles in one season.

A triple double means a player has reached double digits (10 or higher) in three stat categories in a single game. NBA star Russell Westbrook had the most triple doubles ever in one season. In his best game, Westbrook scored 57 points, had 11 assists, and grabbed 13 rebounds!

Who's Number 1?

In the 2020 season, Women's National Basketball Association (WNBA) star Kelsey Mitchell scored a total of 394 points. In the same season, her competitor Diana Taurasi only scored 356 points. Which player was the scoring champ of the season? It was Taurasi! Let's find out why.

Diana Taurasi

Kelsey Mitchell

The Best Average

In basketball, players are **ranked** by their average scores per game, not by season totals. To find the average, the total number of points in a season is divided by the total number of games. Mitchell played 22 games in the 2020 season. So, she averaged 17.9 points per game. Taurasi only played 19 games, so she had a higher average—18.7 points per game.

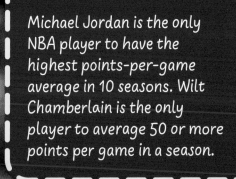

Michael Jordan is the only NBA player to have the highest points-per-game average in 10 seasons. Wilt Chamberlain is the only player to average 50 or more points per game in a season.

Michael Jordan

Wilt Chamberlain

Just 24

The forward is watching the clock. Her team has 24 seconds to take a shot. Her teammates pass the ball around as the clock ticks down. With two seconds left, the forward catches a pass. She turns and shoots just as the buzzer goes off. *Swish!* Two points for her team! But why did they have only 24 seconds to shoot?

A Clock for Speed

In professional basketball, players used to be able to wait as long as they wanted before shooting. But officials wanted to make games more exciting. In the 1950s, a team owner developed a math **formula** to determine the 24-second limit. If a team doesn't take a shot within 24 seconds, the other team gets the ball.

A shot clock above each basket counts down the 24 seconds.

Players have to watch the shot clock to be sure they shoot within 24 seconds.

Do the Math!

It's time to do some basketball math! Learn how to calculate three types of basketball stats. Then, do the math to find out which players had the best stats.

Adding Rebound Stats

Sometimes addition is the best way to get a stat. Add the defensive and offensive rebounds for each player below to find the total.

1. Which player had the most rebounds?

PLAYER	OFFENSIVE REBOUNDS	DEFENSIVE REBOUNDS
Tristan Thompson	226	351
Jarrett Allen	216	455

Free-Throw Shooting Percentages

A percentage is a part of a whole number expressed in hundredths. To find a free-throw shooting percentage, divide the number of times a player made a free throw by the number of attempts. Then move the decimal point two places to the right.

2. Which player was the best at making free throws?

PLAYER	FREE THROWS MADE	FREE THROWS ATTEMPTED
Chelsea Gray	46	49
Skylar Diggins-Smith	90	100

Per-Game Averages

A per-game average shows how well a player did in more than one game. Rebounds and assists are important stats that are counted this way. To find the average, divide the total number of rebounds or assists by the number of games played.

3. Which of these two players had the highest average of rebounds per game?

PLAYER	REBOUNDS	GAMES PLAYED
Hassan Whiteside	905	67
Bam Adebayo	735	72

4. Which player had the highest average of assists per game?

PLAYER	ASSISTS	GAMES PLAYED
Leilani Mitchell	119	22
Alyssa Thomas	101	21

Answers:
1. Thompson had 577 rebounds, and Allen had 671. So, Allen had the most rebounds.
2. Gray was successful at 93.9 percent of her free throw attempts. Diggins-Smith was successful at only 90.0 percent. With her higher percentage, Gray was better at making free throws.
3. Whiteside's average was 13.5 rebounds per game. Adebayo had an average of only 10.2 per game. Whiteside had a higher average.
4. Mitchell's average of 5.4 assists per game is higher than Thomas's average of only 4.8 assists per game.

Glossary

angle the space between two intersecting lines

arc a path that follows a curve

arenas large enclosed buildings used to watch sports or other large events

averages numbers that show how something happened over a longer period of time

backspin the backward rotation of a ball

data information often in the form of numbers

engineered designed using science

force the push or pull of an object

formula a series of steps to solve a math problem

gravity the force that pulls objects toward Earth

high-resolution a type of video that has a large amount of detail

inertia the force that keeps objects at rest or in motion

mass transit transportation systems that move many people at once, such as trains or buses

media websites, TV stations, and newspapers that provide information

ranked placed in order from best to worst

sensors electronic devices that gather and record information

stats short for statistics; information stated as numbers

Read More

George, Enzo. *Physical Science in Basketball (Science Gets Physical)*. New York: Crabtree Publishing Company, 2020.

Havelka, Jacqueline. *STEM in Basketball (Connecting STEM and Sports)*. Broomall, PA: Mason Crest, 2019.

VanVoorst, Jenny Fretland. *The Science Behind Basketball (STEM in the Summer Olympics)*. Minneapolis: Jump!, Inc., 2020.

Learn More Online

1. Go to **www.factsurfer.com**

2. Enter "**STEM Basketball**" into the search box.

3. Click on the cover of this book to see a list of websites.

Index

About the Author

K. C. Kelley has written more than 100 books on sports for young readers, including titles on basketball, soccer, baseball, the Olympics, and much more. He used to work for *Sports Illustrated* and the National Football League.